Beyond Earth:
Jupiter's Moons

Columbus, OH

Front Cover © NASA / Roger Ressmeyer / CORBIS; **3** © Royalty-Free / CORBIS; **7** © NASA; **8-9** © M. Neugebauer / zefa / CORBIS; **10-11** © NASA / Roger Ressmeyer / CORBIS; **12** © PhotoDisc / Getty Images, Inc.; **15** © NASA; **Back Cover** © NASA / Roger Ressmeyer / CORBIS.

SRAonline.com

An Open Court Curriculum.

Printed in China.

Send all inquiries to this address:
SRA/McGraw-Hill
4400 Easton Commons
Columbus, OH 43219

ISBN: 978-0-07-608767-9
MHID: 0-07-608767-0

2 3 4 5 6 7 8 9 NOR 13 12 11 10 09

The McGraw-Hill Companies

The Night Sky

When you gaze at the night sky, what can you see? You can probably see the moon and many stars.

On a very dark night you might detect a fuzzy band of light across the sky. This is part of the Milky Way, our own galaxy.

You may also observe some objects that appear to be very bright stars. Some of these are planets. Mercury, Venus, Mars, Saturn, and Jupiter are all visible to the naked eye. Jupiter is the largest of these.

The shape of the Milky Way galaxy is a great spiral. The sun is in one "arm" of this spiral.

Because of the sun's size, its gravity is very strong. Gravity keeps Earth and the other planets in our solar system in orbit around the sun.

Planets have gravity too. Even though Earth is much smaller than the sun, it has enough gravity to keep you from floating away into space!

Our solar system

Earth's gravity also keeps the moon in orbit around our planet. Saturn's gravity keeps its moons in orbit. It also holds in place the rocks and dust that make up its rings.

Jupiter is the largest planet in our solar system. It has the strongest gravity. Jupiter's gravity holds more than sixty moons in orbit!

Not all planets in our solar system have moons, though. Mercury and Venus don't have moons.

Jupiter is 318 times larger than Earth!

How Is Jupiter Different from Earth?

Compared with the space between stars, the planets in our solar system are close together. Think of our solar system as our neighborhood. Like the people on your street, the planets are all different from one another.

Jupiter and Earth both have a moon or moons, and they both orbit the sun. But they have little else in common. For one thing, Jupiter is made of gases. Earth is solid.

Jupiter's Great Red Spot

Another difference is that Jupiter is many times the size of Earth. To be precise, it is 318 times larger than Earth! Jupiter's Great Red Spot—a huge storm in the planet's atmosphere—is about three times as wide as Earth.

Jupiter spins more than twice as fast as Earth does. Also, Jupiter is farther from the sun. This makes its orbit bigger. It takes Jupiter more than eleven Earth years to go once around the sun.

Could You Live on Jupiter?

People can live on Earth because it is just the right distance from the sun for people, animals, and plants to live. Plants use solar energy to grow. Almost every living thing relies on these plants for food.

Jupiter is much farther from the sun than Earth is. Jupiter is about 391 million miles (629 million km) farther from the sun than Earth. Much less solar energy reaches Jupiter. Even if plants did not need soil, minerals, and oxygen to live, they could not live on Jupiter.

Plants do need soil, though. And so do people. We need something to walk on. The Earth's surface is rocky and firm. The surface of Jupiter isn't solid at all. While scientists think the very center of Jupiter might be solid, most of the planet is made of thick gases.

Also, people and animals need oxygen in the air they breathe. Earth has plenty of oxygen. It also has other gases needed for plants and animals to grow. Jupiter does not have these gases.

Earth's soil and atmosphere are perfect for plants.

Jupiter and its moons: Io (red moon at left) and Europa (white moon at right)

Jupiter's Moons

It may seem odd, but Earth has more in common with Jupiter's moons than with Jupiter itself. Jupiter has more than sixty moons. They are solid and rocky like Earth. But most are small and bare, like Metis, Adrastea, Amalthea, and Thebe. These are the four moons closest to Jupiter.

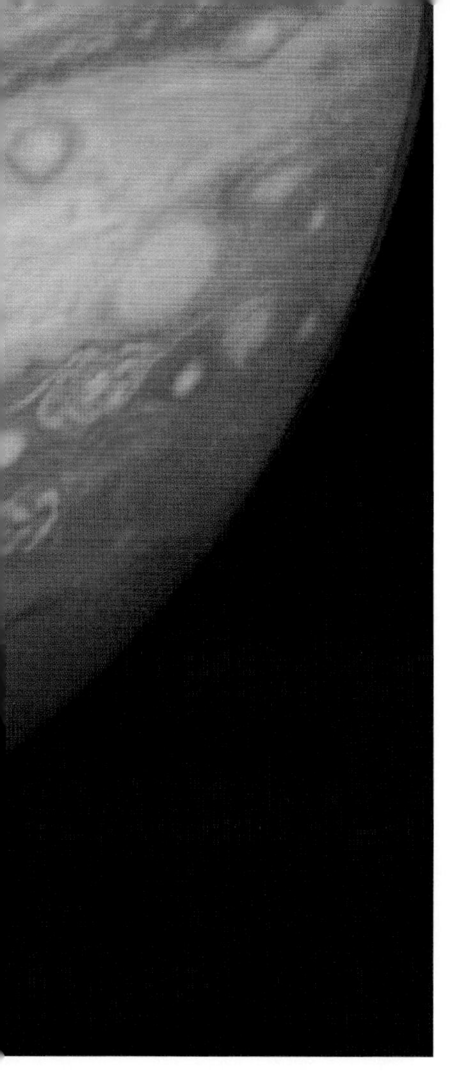

In contrast, the next four are the largest of Jupiter's moons. Io is almost twenty times the size of Amalthea. Europa, Ganymede, and Callisto are each the size of a small planet.

These four planet-sized moons were discovered in 1610. The astronomer Galileo Galilei saw them through his telescope. He saw four bright objects near Jupiter. At first he thought they were stars. Then he noticed they did not move across the sky the same way other stars moved. They were moons!

Many scientists think Jupiter's four largest moons are exciting. Scientists study these moons. Because they are like Earth, the moons can help us learn more about Earth.

Io

Io is the fifth moon from Jupiter. Io's surface is full of volcanoes. They shoot melted rock, ash, and other material high into the air.

Io also has an odd orbit. Its distance from Jupiter varies much more than the other moons. When it is close to Jupiter, Jupiter's gravity pulls on it more. When it is far away, the pull is weaker. These forces cause bulges on Io's surface.

Europa is an interesting moon too. It has one of the smoothest surfaces of any object in our solar system. It is like a smooth ball with fine lines on it.

Europa is made of layers. Europa's crust is made of ice. This icy crust is only about 3 miles (5 km) deep. Under this layer of ice are deep oceans. Scientists think the lines on Europa could be places where the surface has cracked. The cracks fill with water, which freezes over.

Ganymede is the largest of Jupiter's moons. (It is bigger than the planet Mercury!) It is different from many of the moons. Its icy surface has many craters. Like Earth, it has mountains and valleys, hills and ridges.

Scientists sent a space telescope to take pictures of this moon. They were able to detect a little ozone. This is a form of oxygen. There may be a very thin atmosphere that has oxygen around Ganymede!

Callisto is another moon. It has more craters than Ganymede, and its crust has ice. Callisto appears to be very old. Scientists think it is about four billion years old!

You could not live on Jupiter. But could you live on one of its moons? Despite the ways that Jupiter's moons are similar to Earth, scientists have not found life on them. Maybe someday people will visit Jupiter's moons. Maybe it will be you!

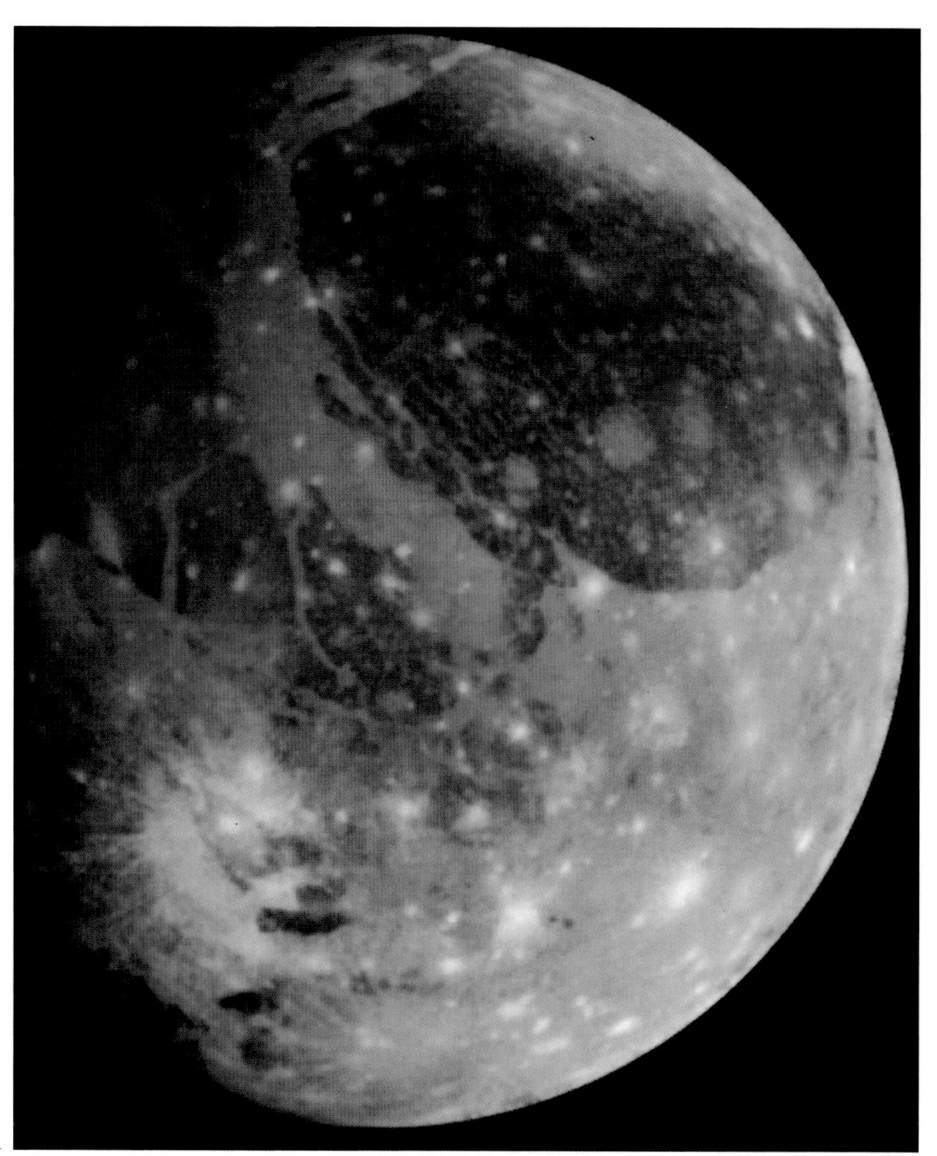

Ganymede's icy surface

Vocabulary

detect (di tekt´) (page 3) *v.* To find out or notice; discover.

galaxy (gal´ ək sē) (page 3) *n.* A very large group of stars.

spiral (spī´ rəl) (page 4) *n.* A curve that keeps winding. A spiral may wind inward and outward or downward and upward.

solar (sō´ lər) (page 4) *adj.* Having to do with or coming from the sun.

precise (pri sīs´) (page 7) *adj.* Exact; definite.

varies (vâr´ ēz) (page 13) A form of the verb **vary:** To change; to make or become different.

bulges (bəl´ jez) (page 13) *n.* Plural of **bulge:** A rounded part that swells out.

Comprehension Focus: Classify & Categorize

1. Name two ways that you can classify Jupiter's moons.
2. Classify each of the following objects as a planet or a moon.
   - Saturn
   - Callisto
   - Ganymede
   - Jupiter
   - Earth